The Words Left Unspoken

ALSO BY ALLIE MICHELLE

Explorations of a Cosmic Soul

The Rose That Blooms in the Night

The Words Left Unspoken

ALLIE MICHELLE

Andrews McMeel
PUBLISHING®

The Words Left Unspoken

Andrews McMeel Publishing
a division of Andrews McMeel Universal
1130 Walnut Street, Kansas City, Missouri 64106

www.andrewsmcmeel.com

23 24 25 26 27 VEP 10 9 8 7 6 5 4 3 2 1

ISBN: 978-1-5248-7863-4

Library of Congress Control Number: 2022945362

Editor: Patty Rice
Art Director: Julie Barnes
Designer: Tiffany Meairs
Production Editor: Meg Daniels
Production Manager: Shona Burns

Cover and interior illustrations by Anfisa Kuzmina

ATTENTION: SCHOOLS AND BUSINESSES
Andrews McMeel books are available at quantity discounts with bulk
purchase for educational, business, or sales promotional use. For
information, please e-mail the Andrews McMeel Publishing Special
Sales Department: sales@amuniversal.com.

For the ones who were silenced. May this book rip off the muzzle and remind you that you have teeth that are meant to sink into the marrow of life. No matter how dark the world becomes, *do not let your light go out.*

I no longer avoid the point of breaking. I say to the world, "Break my heart. Break it so wide open that all of eternity can fit in between the pieces . . ."

Part I: Breaking

a heart that is not hardened
by suffering contains
the kind of love
that turns swords into

f
l
o
w
e
r
s

what are you so afraid of? there are no
failures--it's just life unfolding. sometimes
it will be miraculous, other times it will
be mundane. sometimes you'll be falling in
love, other times you'll be drowning in loss.
sometimes you'll feel high from your dreams
coming true, other times you'll feel hopeless
watching them crumble. it is far better to make
friends with the shadows than run from them.
and so, if you can participate in the whole
of life, and let every experience sculpt your
soul, then no time will ever be wasted. so,
keep going. keep rising and stumbling. keep
following that beating compass in your chest
and finding your way. there's no blueprint
here. all we can do is watch this whole damn
thing unfold and remember that the nature of
life is change. it's our choice to either let
it crash into us or flow through us.

anyone can stand in your light
but few will brave

D
   A
      N
         C
            I
               N
                  G

with your darkness

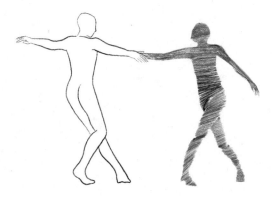

i want to know what it's like for someone to say,
"i love you . . . ?"
without it sounding like a question
to be chosen by someone that
i don't have to second-guess if i should let in
i want to know what it's like not to fall for a lesson
and reassure my heart that them leaving
does not make me less than
i want to know what it's like for "all or nothing"
to not even be an option
because this is not the connection
i need to fear losing or becoming lost in
i want to know what it's like not to hustle for my purpose
and when i don't check off that list
to feel free instead of worthless
i want to know what it's like to be wildly myself
to let my heart guide the way
instead of quieting all it has felt

i didn't know it was you at first
that the universe herself
had arranged our meeting
at that awful New York restaurant
and sitting across from me
was the man who would change my life
you slipped into my heart through the back door
and that place that is normally so guarded
simply opened
as though my heart recognized you
as a part of itself
the first night you held me,
i was shocked that for once
i didn't feel the need to escape
you were home and a grand adventure all at once
everyone looks to you
and i know you wish you could look to him,
but in a world of such brokenness,
you see so simply
how to put the pieces back together again
there's an ocean between us
and i prefer it that way
because i'm terrified that without 3,000 miles of space
you'll find that i'm not the perfect girl you think i am
i've never been fiercely chosen before,
but "maybe" isn't part of your vocabulary
and "no" isn't a word you hear often
so, with a winged heart
i've come to find all that's left to do
is leap with a joyful "yes,"
and whether i fall or fly
it will be with love

WARNING:

Sometimes
The path to a man's heart
Can take a woman
Worlds away from herself . . .

Instead of a swear jar
I'm making an
"I'm sorry" jar
For all the apologies
I have given
Simply for taking up space

when you devote yourself to Love,
ration and reason will disappear
your tongue will become a servant to kindness
as words of sweet truth and compassion
tumble from your lips
no longer will you ask,
"how much can i do with my life?"
but instead,
"how much of life can i notice?"
when you become intimate with Love,
your heart will yank the reins from your mind,
and you may become bruised and battered
from the journey She takes you on,
but without the pain of a hard fall
you wouldn't feel the pleasure of
a courageous heart willing to get back up,
as it beats like a celebratory drum
because you are here
you are still here

Can you say "no" to others
If it means "yes" to your heart?
Can you choose being misunderstood
In the name of not betraying your own soul?
I have never seen radical change
That begins with the act of people pleasing
Transformation is born
When you trust your inner voice
Over a thousand outside opinions

a life that makes perfect sense to everyone else
only exists within a body as pristinely preserved
as a porcelain doll. your movements will be rigid
and linear. the animal skin you wear domesticated,
afraid of your fellow humans. suddenly we pick and
choose which parts of each other to love, chopping
one another to pieces and wondering why we feel so
God damn fragmented. yet the one who embraces their
own beast will never balk from the chaos of another.
it's not that the world is a mirage. it's that we're
staring at the smallest of puzzle pieces assuming
it's the whole picture, wondering why there's this
aching God-shaped hole inside of us that feels like
something is missing.

All that destroys you is a gift
Revealing the only thing you have left
The part of you that is
Indestructible

man is afraid of his own reflection
so he travels from woman to woman
terrified of exploring the depths of one connection
when love is the greatest experience
of being human

hate is the most twisted form of love
i feel it burning inside of me
when i think of what you took
i've never felt so empty
then when i saw how the two of you looked
as though you shared a secret
thinking i was blind
but really i was just
letting the pain strengthen my soul
entertained by all your lies

"i want to marry you," he said to me
"be the mother of my children,"
he said to me
"i'll never leave you," he said to me
i was the love of his life
until he didn't get what he wanted
a year went by
and i had a ring melded from broken promises
that i held with trembling fingertips
as he sat there
waiting for my decision
begging me not to walk away
because he saw what he had too late
"don't let go," he pleaded
words uttered from a dream he had
of his dad
not realizing that i had prayed to his dad
every day for a year
because i didn't want to let go
these words were said to someone else
someone who isn't me
someone who smiled and nodded quietly
as she lay there listening to her partner moan
as he worshipped his assistant next to her
oh well,
at least he wasn't trying to sleep with my sister
  this time
i believed him once
but my heart now knew those words to be hollow

three days after i left
he moved in that same girl
who is now playing wife
in the dream the two of us built
as though i could be so easily erased
so quickly replaced
does she know the stories
of the yellow house you grew up in
with the slanted floor?
and how your spine is out of place
from carrying a family on your back
from such a young age?
does she do cupping,
craniosacral therapy,
acupressure,
reiki,
massage,
cook,
clean,
run a business?
did you ever stop to think
that i was the foundation both of you now stand on?
you look at me like i'm missing out
but a king who forever lost his queen
because he worshipped the idea of "more"
is not the man
i was devoted to
you didn't just hold a heart in your hands
you had *the girl with the heart of all hearts*

one day you'll acknowledge it
one day you'll feel it
until then
keep your *"how are yous"*
i refuse to be disrespected
with such surface conversation
and treated like a stranger
when i gave all of myself over to loving you
forever is a false promise

Give me an honest sinner
Over a lying saint

i'd rather wear my shadow like a cape
than spend my life running away
staying honest with yourself
is a superpower
instead of reaching
for the phone
for the vice
for the success
for the person
for the place
for the food
until you're so numb
you can't even taste
what a waste

is your life even yours
or are you owned
by what you're afraid to face?

stay awake
i'd take an honest sinner
over a lying saint
and denying any part of yourself
is like using only
one color in the palette to paint
when your life was meant
to be a masterpiece
but first you must make peace
with every piece
because light chasing
is a dangerous feat

you offered me gold
in exchange for something
more precious than any metal
but i will never forget
watching you worship her
in all the ways
i had always wanted you to
so, tell me again
how you'll give me a "nice life"
tell me the number that will make up
for my bruised and battered heart
dress my wrists in gold bracelets
so that the sound
of them clanking together
reminds me of what my love is valued at
i'll melt it all down
and give it to you in bricks
for you to build your empty castle with

healing has become a buzzword. a sport in the
spiritual olympics. yet to heal is to be humbled.
to have the confidence to be nothing when we normally
spend every moment attempting to prove we're
something. at first, healing feels a lot like being
at the bottom of the sea with a rock on top of your
chest, wondering when you'll be able to breathe
again. yet sometimes, life knocks the wind out of
our lungs just to remind them how much they enjoy
the taste of air. that which we grieve is that which
we've loved deeply, bringing us intimately in touch
with what it means to be human.

Sometimes the loneliest place to be is in a relationship

i woke up with a heaviness each day
every truth i swallowed started to weigh me down
anchoring me in my own self-deceptions
my conversations became unscripted acting
but my pain would bleed out
in the dark sense of humor
i used as a cry for help
because laughter was my
way of being honest without
having to admit that i had once again
betrayed my own heart
i have a really unique talent
for choosing men who can't choose me
they love to chase me
because my walls are so tall
it's a grand challenge
for them to conquer
until i fall
but they chase me
without being ready to catch me
and so, the walls crumble
leaving my soft heart exposed
but once they have the trophy
of those crumbled bricks
all of a sudden they decide:
this isn't it
i want it all
more money
more houses

more land
more women
more cars
how many mores will be enough
to stop and realize
this is exactly how the world became fucked?

it's never a decision that is hard. it's the in-
between. never quite here, and never quite there.
too scared to lose, and too scared to love. we
avoid the unavoidable in life, when loss is an
inevitable side effect of caring for something
other than yourself. the in-between is more
painful than rejection or failure because *our
hearts are not built to beat halfway.*

Love will bring you to your knees
Until you learn to live your life
In prayer . . .

our emotions are not meant
to hold us back
but help us feel into
the places in our lives
that we hold ourselves back
when rage, sorrow, and despair
come to visit you
shake their hands
and thank them for being
such wonderful friends
they have just handed you
a compass to your healing
your fear is a map to your

F
    R
       E
          E
       D
    O
M

fear and discomfort
are the wings
that carry us closer to truth
strip away those
heavy layers of delusion
that weigh you down
pain is a great teacher
that leaves once she
has taught us what we need to know

this is a love letter to my

S
P
I
N
E

for all the times i laid there
and took it

his love became a collar around my neck
but he dripped it in gold and diamonds
thinking i'd be blinded
and let my leash be just long enough
that i wouldn't even notice
the freedom he would choke from me
every time we fucked
my body was a burial ground for his pain
as though my heart only beat for his gain
so this is a love letter to my spine
for all the times i laid there and took it
the thing about abusive relationships
is most people don't know they're in one
they mistake love for charm and empty promises
your abuser will convince you
that it is your fault
until you start to confuse affection for assault
and love for ownership
even now the freedom on my tongue
has an aftertaste of guilt
for not being the perfect wife
in the dream that he built
everywhere i went
he would find me
and remind me
that he still held my leash
except now i laugh in his face
and wear that collar as a crown
because when he tried to bury me
i became the queen who rose from the ground

bow to your struggles
they are the boiling water
that turns your heart tender
they are the fire that forges
you into a blade of truth
they are the harsh winds
that crumble all falsehoods
they are the earth grounding you
in what it really means to be
h
u
m
a
n

how do you know the difference
between love and infatuation?
infatuation tastes only
the surface of your light,
love knows the part of you
no one else does
both sacred and secret
like the dark side of the moon . . .

trust is not built by maintaining a front of
perfection. trust is made up of the small moments
that we reveal our imperfections. no soul yearns
to embrace a flawless mirage, but rather to walk
hand in hand with someone who has gotten their
nails dirty digging into their depths. someone
who has been banged up by taking the unpaved path
and earned their wisdom by being brave enough
to make mistakes. trust is not built by never
wronging another, but by how we atone for our
wrongdoings. trust is the willingness to show up,
not when things are going smoothly, but in the
difficult times that we are barely able to hold
ourselves upright and say, "i will catch you. i
will always catch you." how ironic, that we think
the most vulnerable and messy places in us are
unworthy of love, when those uniquely human quirks
are exactly what we fall for. when will we realize
that transparency is the birthplace of trust?

i'm not her anymore
a doll
you can dress up
and leave on the shelf
when you've had enough
you call yourself a god
but your actions speak of a god
i don't recognize
i tried to draw out
the real one who hides inside
but it nearly destroyed us both
i was no longer a perfect ideal
but an imperfect real
how ironic that
you were not my jailer
it was always me
it's funny how we imprison ourselves
yet still hold the key

death makes all of life sacred,
and what is the meaning of sacred
but that which is holy?
there is nothing in existence
the divine has not kissed

Holy = Whole

(to embrace the opposing forces within)

Gratitude isn't a list in our minds, or a hollow
word tossed around. Gratitude is the full
participation of life--a meeting of the moment
exactly as it is. We embody gratitude each time we
really taste our food, let music flood our soul,
or appreciate the warmth of another person's hands
interlaced in ours. Gratitude isn't a denial of
our challenges but choosing to use adversity as
an instrument that reshapes us for the better.
The secrets are always hidden in the simplest
of places, found only by those who truly see
through eyes of wonder. As you think of each part
of your life you are thankful for, lose yourself
in it for a moment. Become it. Feel it all. And
most importantly, instead of searching for the
way, take the unknown's hand and dance with it.

there is a difference between blame and boundaries
blame plays victim and loudly yells, "this is your fault!"
but boundaries and compassion are married
they tenderly interlace hands and say
"thank you for the lesson
i hold nothing but love for you in my heart
but you are no longer welcome here"

nothing is holding you back
nothing ever has
your shackles are not shackles
they are your own hands clasped together
pick up the sword of truth
and slay your "i can'ts"
and your "i shoulds"
why live beneath such a low ceiling
when your roof could be
the entire universe?

those moments when we're squirming beneath our
skin with discomfort, the brave ones plant their
feet firmly in the ground because they know the
fear of pain is worse than the moment of pain
itself. and the further we run, the bigger the
shadows chasing us seem. what if we stopped
splitting ourselves apart with good sides and bad
sides, but chose to welcome all sides? exiling the
messy places in ourselves is like listening to
a song composed of only one note, expecting it to
be a grand symphony. take a second, i mean
truly pause and ask yourself, "what am i running
from?" *if you learn what you're running from, you
may just discover what you were born to run toward.*

having expectations of your lover
is like choking them
and then asking
why they aren't breathing

at some point, we are no longer mirages
interacting with each other, pretending to have
it all figured out. at some point, you'll begin
to recognize everyone as utterly human. your
teachers are not masters. your lovers are
flawed. your friends are messy. your heroes are
vulnerable. at some point, you'll begin to see the
little kid in everyone. the one who is curious, a
little afraid, and seeking to love and be loved.
it is at this point that we become liberated. we
become disentangled from our expectations of one
another, finally able to feel we are not alone.
because life is short and death is long. so, it
is far better to explore the questions hand in
hand, joined together by uncertainty.

We yearn for connection, yet isolate ourselves.
We seek love, but fear loss. We dream for someday,
instead of trying for today. We want change,
but don't want to change. We overconsume, then
wonder why there's no space to create. We love
the ocean, yet pollute its waters. We advocate
for education, then bury our students in loans.
We want health, but for a price. We believe in
equality, but struggle to bridge the gap of
inequality. We ask for better leaders, but don't
think to lead. We wish for a better world, but
not at the cost of comfort and convenience.
We are walking contradictions. There's a
disconnect here. And it's not any one person's
fault. The world is made up of both beauty and
brokenness. Most of the time, I believe we have
our hearts in the right place. The problem is how
overwhelming it all seems, but change is made up
of small moments. Change happens when we have
been hurt, but choose not to act from our hurt.
Change happens when we don't pretend to have
all the answers, but are willing to ask the
uncomfortable questions. The truth is, if we knew
the whole story behind everyone's actions, we
would see why they are the way they are. And
it doesn't excuse it, but compassion is the
birthplace of change.

the experiences we want
to be saved from
oftentimes offer
the most sacred of lessons

Every time you look to ease your pain
Numbing yourself with that vice
You claim has no effect
Know that I feel everything you don't
Know that every justification that pours out of your mouth
Is the poison I choke on
It took me a while to realize
The magic you showed me was only a sleight of hand
You act like you're hard
Like the world has no effect on you
But the soft hearts around you are crumbling
From your effect on them
They told me all you needed was a reason to live
And yet the teacher who preaches the medicine he could
  never swallow
Is only a con artist
Now that, I'll admit, you're the best at
You even fooled yourself
They told me I became your reason to live
And I felt the weight of that crush my spine
Even though I knew it was a lie
You have no reason to live
Because addiction is like watching someone you love
Stab their own heart in slow motion
While you have no choice but to watch them bleed out
Until their very last breath

when all is spinning
out of control
the only sensible thing to do
is laugh louder than God
until she calms this chaotic world
just to hear what's so funny

"there's a reason there aren't more female CEOs,"
he says without meeting my eyes
i swallow the disgust that climbs up my throat
ready to turn itself into rage
and spit words of flame
that would turn
his inflated ego to ash
i want to say
that his mother issues
are leaking from behind that thick
mask of masculinity
that the only thing he's capable
of multitasking
is having one hand to jerk himself off
and the other watching his self-worth
rise and fall with his Bitcoin account
but i know i have to play his game
in order to change the rules
so, i take in his smug expression
and smile sweetly
as i let him lecture me
on how to run my business
because while he listens to himself talk
i'm building an empire
built by women
who don't use words like,
"either,"
"or,"
it's always, "and"
because we can bear our children

and build a business
before he can even finish
his speech
when you give to get
your love will always be in debt

rage came to visit me
and i greeted her like an old friend
she looked at me
with pain in her eyes
and said, *"where have you been?"*
i dissociated so that i wouldn't
have to associate with the pain
but the thing about shadows
is they follow anyway
"STAY,"
i beg myself
"don't be afraid of what you haven't felt"
suppression is a building block
for depression
and i had so many blocks i couldn't breathe
so, i jump-started my heart
and drove straight through
my own walls
because i am here to catch
myself now if i fall
the ironic thing about presence
is that when you're here
i mean *really here*
there's nothing to fear
the monster is birthed
in our minds
and i am sick and tired
of saying, "everything's fine!"
the mess is what's perfect

so upholding a facade
will never be worth it
and the thing about pain
is that
your healing is matched
by the depth of your feeling

It's not time that heals all wounds. It's love over
    time.

every day she stood there with her heart
in her hand and asked,
"will you accept this?"
but his back was turned
as he looked toward all the
other possibilities of what could be
trying on different songs to hear which one
he wanted to dance to
but he didn't realize that the rhythm of her heartbeat
was a song she sung only for him each day
that told the tale of their love
the music of her devotion
a year went by
and she grew so very tired
and on the last day she offered it to him
with shaking hands
his back was still turned
so, she placed it back in her own chest
he turned around after she left
but the song had already begun to change
and so, he heard the music of her love
when it was too late
he fought for her hard and true
to win the devotion
that had already been broken
this tale is sad
but not hopeless
they rose in love
they rose in their dreams
they rose in destiny

but they were not
each other's to keep
and now their love
can rest in peace

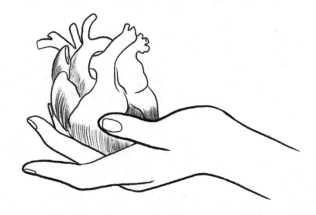

Whatever you clutch the tightest is usually what
you're meant to let go of first.

I'll say it again

Whatever you clutch the tightest is usually what
you're meant to let go of first . . .

lost is a bridge to the soul. instead of reaching
to claim that you belong to something, some place,
or someone, if you can step atop that wobbling
bridge and walk inside of yourself, you may find
that your greatest expansion comes from the
experiences your heart wants to contract around
the most. grief, loneliness, failure, betrayal,
heartbreak--these are some of life's most potent
seasonings for the soul if we allow them to
ferment in us. a life of absolute certainty is
flavorless. the mystic willingly dies a thousand
deaths because they know the cost of the life that
is meant for them is the life they thought they
were supposed to have . . .

it doesn't matter how they see you
how do you see you?
would you deny becoming
who you are meant to be
for the approval of others
when you only occupy a
few magic seconds of eternity?

i heard Love laughing
at all my plans
that i thought were so grand
She saw me hunched over
my life's canvas
painting with white knuckles
only creating more struggle
i finally turned to Her
hair messy and eyes wild
in a frenzy of my own worries
She smiled and said,
"when will you realize
you were meant to be the paintbrush
not the painter?"
and so i surrendered my body
into Love's hands
and let Her use me
so the real masterpiece
could begin

Shed your skin
Until you meet
The soul within

When I see you,
I smile and say,
"How are you?"
But what I really want to do
Is lay out all the messages I never sent
I would have an entire novel
That I would call *Unspoken*
I would tell you that I miss
The smell of your skin
And how I would forget
Who I am
Or where I've been
As I melted away at your touch
I would tell you that I miss
Wrapping my legs around you
Every morning to hold you in bed
Just a little bit longer
Before you started work
I was your anti-alarm clock
Because I knew our cuddles
Were the best part of the day
I would tell you about the countless nights I spent
In our living room
Scribbling in my journal
Reasons why you shouldn't walk away
As you shut down
And I wanted to bang my fists against your chest
Until the doorway to your heart opened again
I would tell you that I hated cooking
But found myself spending hours
Looking for recipes
Because it was worth it to bring you pleasure

And watch your face as you felt my love
In every taste
I would tell you how angry I am
That you saw what you had too late
And gave it all away
I would tell you that I can't talk to you
Because all I see is the kids
We would have had
With big red hair and freckles
Sprinkled across their faces
Like a constellation
Our boy probably would have been
An emotional poet
And our little queen
A ruthless businesswoman
Following in her daddy's too big footsteps
I would tell you that I let go of us
A little more each day
Because I see how much better we are now
But if I'm being honest
I would tell you that the ring you gave me
Is still collecting dust
In the corner of my room
Because I can't bring myself to throw it away
And once someone is part of your heart
They will be forever
So, when I see you
I choke on all these words
Swallow the truth
And ignore the lump in my throat
Smile and say,
"How are you?

Part II: Becoming

this is your reminder to rip off the muzzle.
you have teeth that are meant to sink into the
marrow of life. you are not here to shape-shift
your identity to belong or be digestible, because
if they cannot swallow their own chaos, they will
always shrink from yours. this is your reminder
that security is too steep a price to trade for
your wildness, and you are far too magnificent to
be domesticated by handing over that thundering
heart to anyone else. so, let freedom rip from
your vocal cords as you howl at the moon weaving
future memories with your words. *sing the truth of
the tucked-away corners of your heart and never
again let them tuck you away.* my dear, this tug-of-
war of being too much or not enough is the most
exhausting work in the world, and i need you awake
to dance with me, hair unbound and feet bare
beneath the dark night as the stars perform for
those who remember their sacred wild.

this is the secret:
keep your heart in wonder
and you will resist nothing
by resisting nothing
you will experience everything
your pain will be the growing pains
of a soul willing to stretch
your joy will be the joy
of knowing that your life was lived sincerely
and never again will you question
if you are meant to go right or left
because a wondrous heart knows
the path is wherever they step

the woman who treats herself as a queen
has her chin held high
and her heart wide open
she cannot be brought to her knees
because she already lives her life
in prayer
the woman who feels the most
contains the most life
the most wisdom
she understands her emotions
to be the language of spirit
speaking through her
the woman who honors and respects
her inner voice
over any outside opinion
who follows it with relentless grace
the woman who honors her body
as a portal between two worlds
who understands it to be a direct line to God
and does not allow it to become an escape
or burial ground for the pain of others
the woman who seeks counsel
from every generation of women
she treasures their voices
and hears their wisdom
the woman who understands
the power of surrender
who allows her life to unfold
with divine intelligence

and trusts her soul
in painting its own path
this woman is a queen
it's you
and it's me

If you want a conscious man who honors you, then
you have to own the ways you have unconsciously
dishonored yourself. To reclaim your pleasure, you
must reclaim your pain. Once you own every inch
of who you are, nothing and no one can own you.
Look inside and hold your little girl close, and
she will show you how to look through the eyes
of an awakened woman. See the times you sought
your lover's attention instead of finding home
within your own. The times you played the healer
or the mother to prove your love was needed. The
times you looked to him to fill the father role
your younger self needed. The times you clung to
a future promise for a false sense of security
to place a bandage on top of every underlying
insecurity. The times your hard "no" became a
soft "yes." The times you let your instincts be
silenced through his persistent explanation. I
know it's hard, my love, but reclaim all of it. Feel
all of it, because the woman who feels the most
contains the most life. So shake up the power that
sleeps inside of you and let it burst. Surrender
to yourself and trust that you will not fall
apart. On the other side isn't just pleasure, but
divine pleasure. It isn't just love, but divine
love. If you want a conscious man who honors you,
fiercely honor yourself first.

the body
a sacred temple
feet bruised from wandering the galaxy
legs that carry her with a strength
that makes mountains quiver
hips that house the womb that births new worlds
a heart that speaks the wordless language of love
breasts that showed the earth
how to design its own curvature
arms that hold each moment tenderly as a newborn
hands marked with lines
that are a remembrance of those who came before her
a throat crafted with a voice
that sings the truth of the ancients
lips made from the petals of a rose
freckles sprinkled from fallen stars
eyes blazing with the fire of the sun
hair that falls fluid as water
bone and flesh that hold all of infinity
the body
a sacred temple
did you forget it was anything else?

Every second that passes is an exchange. You're filling in the blank pages of your life that you will never get back. The way you spend your moments shapes the way your story turns out. Maybe you don't control the characters or the plot twists, but you're the writer--a fact that is both empowering and paralyzing. The great internal battle is to stay aware, so you don't wake up at 75 and realize you lost precious chapters of your story to an apathetic sleep. So, pick up the pen. What tale is worth the exchange of time?

i woke up and peered out my window
into the dark night
and saw an angel and a devil standing there
the angel's robes were perfect and pristine
never touched by the suffering of humanity
and the devil had forgotten
what it was like to have wings
that the only way to fly
is to let go of the weight of his pain
there i sat
watching what i thought of
as black and white turn gray
as their lips met
beneath the starry sky
and it was then
that i saw
an angel and a devil
fall in love
beyond all notions of good and evil
there is only love and the absence of love
the angel's wings dissolved
the devil transformed before my eyes
and they were utterly human
heaven and hell are not two separate places
but dwell within the soul
so i turned away from the window
and passed my demons a drink
and they told me of compassion
that to love the darkness in another

i must first hold my own as sacred
because without a little
heaven and hell in us all
we wouldn't know the glory of what it means
to be human

when you go in search of a master
life will send a thousand jokers dressed as gurus
in a crowd of preachers shouting the answers
you'll find the real one hidden in the corner,
laughing at this circus of illusions

How many lives had to be lived
For you to even be born?

what are you more afraid of?
failure or success?
if i were to guess
i would say we're all terrified of success
because playing victim to your circumstance
is a lot easier than taking a chance
and dancing with your destiny
but why else are we here?
and let me make it clear:
success isn't a milestone
it's a perspective
i covered my eyes
so i wouldn't be blinded
by my own light
because if i shine too bright
i'm afraid everyone will leave
but i'm learning that who i really am
is far more interesting
than who anyone wishes me to be
you see, playing small is like a tree
that refuses to provide oxygen to the world
because it feels unworthy of its own existence
now who does that help?
how many lives had to be lived
for you to even be born?
really think about it
how many lives had to be lived
for you to even be born?
the very fact that you are still here

is your permission slip of worthiness
just look down at your body
and you will see a walking poem
written by millions of years of evolution
home is a place within your own bones
and heaven dwells within your soul
i suppose that's the game of being human,
we forget
to remember
that we're already whole
but that gaping God-shaped hole
we try to fill with distraction
is meant to be left empty
because it's the birthplace of creation
and the unknown
is the only place that has air
for the divine to breathe
so the choice is yours
you can master self-sabotage and being a victim
or you can stand tall, dust off those old stories
and see how far you can run
without the chains of limiting beliefs shackled to
  your feet
because as you liberate yourself
you remind everyone else
how much they, too, enjoy being free

longing is the long walk
home to your heart . . .

but i had bruises on my feet
from running so far away from myself
it takes 200 muscles
just to take one step
and yet i stubbornly
crawled toward discomfort
because i thought it was the blade
that would sculpt my soul
and i wanted to prove
i could turn a sword
into a flower
every time we fall in love
we exchange a piece
of our heart with another
so that by the time
death greets us
like an old friend
we're filled with pieces
from all the lives that touched us
creating a beginning at the end
because *as we return to the earth*
we become the ground
our descendants will dance on
we avoid the unavoidable in life
but i want my heart to break
so wide open
all of eternity can fit
in between the pieces
only when i was blinded enough

to look through the eyes of my heart
did i finally meet myself
back at the start
so, longing is a road map for belonging
and connection is your loneliness set free
all of this sounds poetic and nice
so i have to tell you the truth now
about this thing called life
only step on Love's path
if you're willing to lose
because pain is a side effect
of caring for someone other than yourself
but let it carve and dig into you
until you become empty as the night
because an instrument that is full
cannot create music
and God has been holding Her breath
waiting to sing through you

what if everything you spoke happened instantly?
would you ever judge or gossip again,
knowing your voice
wove instant webs of truth?
Love sewed poetry onto my tongue
so that each word that tumbled
from my lips
would provide understanding
for the misunderstood hearts in this world
but a real master does not need
to speak at all
one look into their eyes
would flood you with so much compassion
you could quench the thirst for Love
for everyone in existence

i couldn't sleep the other night
i curled up in bed and put a mask over my eyes
took my breath in counts of five
but kept falling into black holes
inside of my mind
i turned on one of those bedtime stories
a rendition of *Beauty and the Beast*
he whisks her away to a castle
locks her in a tower and pins her wings
until she learns to love her captor
and flying becomes a distant memory
what they never told me
was that the beast is not a prince
he lives inside of me
the voice in my mind that panics
anytime i feel joy
because the other shoe is bound to drop,
right?
people try to pass me candles
light the way with their advice
what they don't realize
is i'm not afraid of the dark
i'm afraid that when my light comes back
the beast will steal it for himself
shred it to ribbons with claws and fangs
because letting me
outside that castle
isn't safe
"how are you?"
"what did you do today?"

my conversations feel like
speaking into a glass vase
i desperately want to shatter into
a thousand pieces
as an honest laugh finally escapes me
but black roses have bloomed from my shoulder
their vines wrapping around my throat
choking the truth from my vocal cords
so, i make my voice soft
tug the corners of
my mouth into a slight smile
until i look like her
like the Beauty they always knew
it took me a while to realize
that "once upon a time"
is not the fairy tale of my life
so, i crossed out "happily ever after"
and decided that
this is a story
where Beauty learns to love
her own beast
my *softness* is my *strength*
so it's time i love both parts of me

love is choosing to stay
when everything in you wants to run
love is choosing to admit your pain
when everything in you wants to lash out
love is choosing to let go
when everything in you wants to hold on
love is choosing not to fix
but instead to feel
and love is choosing the imperfect real
over a perfect ideal

After observing the earth for many years, the
stars turned to the moon and asked, "How do they
not understand how short their precious lives are?
Why do they waste time doing anything but that
which makes their sweet hearts come alive?" The
moon smiled softly, "Some of them still do. The
artists, the poets, the dreamers, the seekers.
They feel it, and dedicate their whole lives to
trying to capture the beauty of the world from
their first breath to their last." The stars looked
down and saw a woman in the grass with a canvas,
painting them as they watched over her. They began
to dance for her, slowly shooting across the sky
and reflecting the spark in her eyes as she rushed
to paint their magnificence. The moon smiled and
shined a bit brighter, "For the ones who remember
to look up."

Your skin is the closest I've come
To touching God

alone is the only time
my heart isn't on loan . . .
i've experienced far too many men
open a heart they can't hold
they either want to force me into their fairy tale
or fuck me to fulfill their fantasy
either way
they leave no air for me to breathe
and they'll say all the "perfect things"
with an undertone of something else entirely
as though a woman's intuition can't see through
those pretty lies they speak
what he thinks i want to hear
is not honey dripping from his lips
it's poison to my ears
the irony is if he gave me the whole truth
he'd get everything he wants
and i would open for him like
a flower constantly in bloom
and he wouldn't just get his idea of me
the woman who wakes him up
in the middle of the night
pulling him from one dream into another
the woman he is someday
proud to call wife
the mother of his children
a lifelong best friend
i am all wrapped into one
here to unravel him

i'll treat his body like a prayer
as i worship it with my tongue
his skin is the closest
i'll come to touching God
so i'll take my time making him come
for me
but for now
i'll wait alone
because it's the only time
my heart isn't on loan
i'm ready for a man
who isn't here to sell me on a dream
but gives me the gift
of brutal honesty
so to all the little boys
playing God
i say take a number
and get in line
come back when you're ready
to dive deep into the divine
and feel infinite
within our finite lives
because that is the only thing
i'll accept in mine

The moment we claim we own something
Is the moment we become owned
The three greatest lies
Are death
Time
And mine

I once looked into a mirror of shadows
Meant to test the strength of the soul
It reflected every piece of me
I had not made peace with
that kept me from feeling whole
The looking glass showed me the worst,
All those messy and unlovable parts
The ways in which I hurt and was hurt,
But contrast is required in any work of art
Those who love honestly
Are never dishonest with themselves
They do not expect to live flawlessly
For perfection is its own kind of hell
I recognize those who looked into the mirror
By the twinkle of humor in their eyes
They are the ones who were brave enough to heal
And remember *all that is not love is a lie*

(The only way to see yourself is to look at the
  reflection inside)

relationships can quickly become a sinking ship
if you don't know what
your heart wants going into it
on one hand
there are monogamous relationships
that create an encagement of forever
until you're sleepwalking
with a false sense of security
and wake up in your 60s
saying,
"wait, this isn't me anymore."
on the other hand
there's polyamory
built on peter pan syndrome
that buries attachment issues
within the suit of sovereignty
on an insatiable quest for more
until "more" becomes your master
and you travel from person to person
just to avoid your own reflection
so what are we to do?
i took both hands
placed them on my heart
and begged for clarity
the answering beat
was like a drum of laughter
every *thump thump* a reminder
that the more my mind
tries to figure out what love is

the more i am only shown what it is not
because a prince may pick you
up in a carriage
that can quickly become a cage of conditions
but the king of kings knows to
look through the eyes of his heart
because vulnerability
is the safest place to be
when you're walking alongside a true queen
i love you
and you love me
everything after that
is extra noise
however you paint your dream of together
is ultimately your choice
but the only way to know the way
is to ask yourself:
am i committing to a person
or to love itself?

there's a plant called the stinging nettle
its tips kiss your skin and bleed poison
yet the very same vine offers leaves of medicine
are we not the same?
we give what we have an excess of
pain or pleasure
bitterness or bliss
greed or gratitude
cruelty or compassion
life may bury you
and yet your soul is the seed
that will rise from the ground
watered by what is overflowing
from your cup
you are the poison and the medicine
both are as necessary
to the balance of life
as day and night
what would happen
if we stopped trying to feel better
but instead got better at feeling?
you are the poison and the medicine
remember
an open heart is the safest place to be
it is the only thing big enough
to contain all the paradoxes of humanity
there is no need to avoid being burned
when you become the fire you once feared

the moon and i have become great friends
every night we curl up with a blanket of stars
and discuss this exquisite game of being human
we listen to each wild beating heart
like the ticking of a clock
marking the moments of every precious life
we laugh as they all run around
trying to get somewhere
desperately seeking a grand finale
to their life's song
when they could have danced
to every note both high and low
letting the music move through them
when dawn breaks
the sun comes to sit with us
for the one part of the day
that he can be with the moon
when it's neither dark nor light
but the colors that bleed in between
i ask him what the day will bring
how will life break my heart open today?
will i be brought to my knees, or will i grow wings?
is there some great love or death,
some failure or success that will occur?
the sun and the moon laugh
knowing that if i had the answers
i would stop dancing
and what would life be
in a world without music?

what if it's all perfect? the moments when it feels
like you're at the bottom of the sea, being held
down by life with a rock on top of your chest,
wondering when you'll reach the surface again. the
moments when your dreams are coming true, and
it feels like your fluttering heart will take
flight from your rib cage. the moments when you
feel unbelievably lost and can't find a reason to
anchor why you're here. the moments when you're
as intimate with purpose as the sun is with the
earth. the moments when you feel so confident
nothing can touch you. the moments when you feel
so fragile even a single look crumbles you. what
if the experience of these moments is the whole
point? they don't define us, but they do deepen the
well of our spirit, allowing us to overflow with
more life. the only mistake would be to think any
of it lasts. and so, from this place, we have only
the choice of our response: open or close. harden
or soften. feel or numb. break or break open.

what else are we here to do with these
wild beating hearts but love?

there was a pandemic in my heart that said,
"keep six feet apart."
every poem i wrote was laced with bitter pain
from the poison i was too afraid to let bleed out
but the venom we hold in
spreads invisibly beneath our skin
and the separation only isolated me
from who i truly wanted to be
stripped bare of all my armor
left naked from the inside out
because i wasn't built for battle
my heart resides on both sides
so now i wear my flaws
like a badge of honor:
hi
i'm allie
i should probably warn you i'm not perfect
in case you haven't figured that out
i'm a dramatic poet
with a dark sense of humor
who is stubborn as hell
i get lost spiraling in my mind sometimes
with insecurity and doubt
and am like a tornado in the kitchen
my dad always tells me that i stick my finger
in the air
to see which way life's winds will blow me that day
and it's true
i'll flip my world upside down in an instant

for the sake of my heart
because it is the greatest compass
i have ever known
so, i'll always keep you on your toes
and only demand you
come as you are
i'll love your joy
i'll love your sorrow
i'll love your anger
i'll love your passion
i'll love your fear
i'll love your laugh
i'll kiss your tears
there is nothing excluded in me
so, i'm here to welcome all of you
to celebrate your light
and dance with your darkness
as we laugh together
at how we once looked at life
through the lens of two

My lungs were the first thing God kissed
When I came into this world
So every inhale
And exhale
Is a love story of purpose

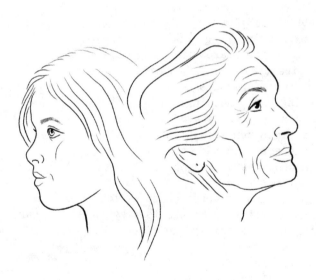

i'm light on my feet
already halfway out the door
before i've even walked in
because if i'm here long enough
to put my full weight into the ground
i'll sink into the moment like quicksand
my friends tell me that
i should have been a magician
i've never once pulled
a rabbit out of a hat
but my disappearing act
will make you scared to blink
it's like trying to catch mist
with your fingertips
grasping for something
that can never be yours
i sometimes wonder
how the space in the room
feels about me occupying it
i sometimes wonder
if the ground is upset about my footsteps
why do we act like humble is a synonym for shame?
when humble is really the wisdom
not of who we are
but *whose* we are
as i commit to love
i find myself in the face of everything but
when i start a relationship with a man
i analyze him under a microscope

so i can know
all the pitfalls
before i free fall
into him
even when we're skin to skin
i'm miles away because i know
that if i get too close
i'll shave off my edges
until i've folded myself
to fit into him
like a beautiful ghost
i introduce him to my roommates
anxiety and depression
so he knows who i've been living with
for a lifetime
they're messy
they don't clean up after themselves
sometimes they're so loud
i can't sleep or know a moment's peace
but still, i show him
i show him
so he knows
that when i look like i've swallowed
the sun with my smile
who is waiting in the shadows
i'm sculpting the woman
i'm becoming from clay
but if i'm honest i don't know
whose hands are doing the molding

as a thousand fingerprints
are left on my pulsing bleeding heart
and my body curls around him
like a question mark
as i lay there
wondering who the fuck i am
but still
i refuse to lose the invisible battle
this poem reveals
still
i refuse to close my heart
so instead i close my eyes and
whisper these secrets into the dark
until it echoes back a promise
yes
it is safe
it is safe to be here
just be here

I will tell you the secret
To never worrying about
Making the "right choice" again
If it is done from love
It will be done rightly
So why don't we just take those reins
And pass them to the heart for a while
She has been aching to be let out
Of those caged ribs

the original meaning of the word weird
w
y
r
d
was destiny
meaning
to be weird is to be one who follows
the path of their destiny
meaning
that normal is a clear road that has already been
  paved
and when you're wyrd
no one else can show you the way
what is my destiny?
i can't help but wonder
what i'm even doing here sometimes
i go about my life on autopilot
and forget that i'm alive
is the point to work?
to hustle for my purpose
check off that list of to-dos
so i don't feel worthless?
is it to find "the one?"
fall in love
create a family
until death decides to come?
or maybe it's to fight
in the battleground of my mind
at the past that tries to take hold of me

and i ignore the way my heart stops when
i trip over my own thoughts
at the sound of your name
i'll smile
when i tell the story of how i transcended it all
how much it all taught me
how i did enough ceremonies
and wrote enough poems to
walk on water
wearing pristine robes
but
nowadays
i think i'd rather wear a black cloak
so my shadow becomes my cape
and everyone around me can embrace
being gloriously human
they can fuck
and dance
and smoke
and eat
and rise
and stumble
and fall to their knees
my lungs were the first thing God kissed
when I came into this world
so every inhale and exhale
is a love story of purpose
so i hope you're wyrd like me
one on the path of their destiny

You are a mystery I could spend
My whole life unraveling

i would have loved you
in another life
when the time was right
i would have sat with you
beneath the haven of those sleepless nights
watching you find the exhale you crave
in the snowy powder spilled across the table
i would have laughed as i watched you
dig into everyone around you until dawn
flipping peoples' perspectives upside down
looking for yourself
i would have felt you melt into my touch
as we found home in a different kind
of pleasure
than either of us had ever known
you're the magi in the corner
who never shows all the cards up his sleeve
but i have been playing with that deck
for lifetimes
you appeared the fool
but i immediately saw God dressed as a joker
perhaps the greatest comedy yet
is being denied the one dance partner
who could have swirled through eternity laughing
  at this circus of illusions with me
we both love being the healer
but you can't save someone
who is already the medicine
so, the thing about a perfect mirror

is that you can never touch the reflection
so, i would have loved you
but if i did
the mirror would shatter
ending both of our games
and what else is there to do
but play this wild game of Love?
so, i would have loved you
but you wisely chose to turn away
from the mirror
maybe in the next lifetime we won't be so wise
and we'll get to dance again right here

the in-between. a strange yet sacred place to
be. when one chapter of life has closed, and the
next has yet to begin. it feels like living
through a moment-to-moment cliff-hanger. the in-
between. home to immense longing and loneliness,
both of which are necessary materials to build
the bridge from who we once were to who we're
becoming. we often resist that wobbly bridge with
every uncertain step. how many times will we trade
the in-between for distraction, and face that
dreaded question: do we chase the ghost of the
life we had, or hungrily claw for a purpose by
seeking a new project, place, or person? the key
is to become intimate with the emptiness like
it were part of our own rib cage. to bravely go
forth into how we feel because every tear is
a reminder of our humanity and every bit of
laughter is a triumphant celebration. so strip
yourself down. shed your skin until you meet the
soul within. get to know the voices in your head.
make friends with them. give them room without
giving them the sails of your ship because the
rarest stars only come out in the darkest of
nights. treasure the in-between. *if you think
all you are is who you could be, you'll never
experience your own divinity.*

PART III: Unbecoming

You are half God
And half earth
Remind me again
Why you ever questioned your worth

the wise ones will tell you not to search for
purpose, or love, or success. in fact, they'll
tell you not to search for anything at all.

instead they'll say,
"did you notice? did you notice the way dawn broke
that day? did you notice the song of the wind as
it whistled through your ears? did you notice the
light that danced in your lover's eyes when they
laughed? did you notice the smell of the flowers
you walked past? did you notice? did you notice
the way your best friend shook with grief as you
held them, and a river of tears poured from their
eyes? did you find the rare stars that only come
out in the dark night, or did you spend all
your time rushing to get to the light? did you
cradle each moment with tender care? or were you
blinded by that joker we call potential, to
the millions of tiny perfect moments we wove
together just for you. did you notice?"

chaos was the compass
i navigated the world with
dancing beneath
the thunder that beat
loud as my own heart
purple clouds swirl about
lightning goes
flash flash flash
and i race toward the rain
because
all that i
once feared
i now love

when you move about life
bracing for impact
preparing for a possible storm
until you're wound up
in knots bound
by invisible worries
life will pull the strings
of your self-control
thread by thread
until the only thing
you have left to hold onto
is trust

they tell me of the beauty
of becoming
and i just smile
with that fire sparkling
in my eyes
because they don't yet know
the ecstasy you find
in unbecoming

Free yourself from the burden of trying to get it right
Instead
Seek experiences that force your spirit to

S

    T

        R

           E

              T

                C

                    H

The golden handcuff

The golden handcuff is when something is so comfortable, so nice and familiar, that it becomes difficult to leave. Yet that very sense of security becomes a shackle that keeps us from stepping forward and stretching our spirit. We pretend not to know. We stay past the expiration date. That relationship we kind of think is right, that job we kind of like working, that place we kind of like living. Until suddenly, we're "kind of" living our lives. Our hearts are not built to beat halfway. To break the golden handcuff is terrifying. It feels like our life is turning upside down and we're suddenly thrust into the unknown. Yet why else are we here, other than to wholeheartedly participate with the mystery as it unfolds? Any redirection is an act of grace. Whether we suffer or surrender is entirely up to us. So, what is your golden handcuff?

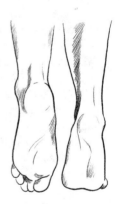

The last trap

The last trap is a way of using spirituality to
exile anyone or anything that doesn't squeeze
into our image of a life of spirit. Phrases like,
"They're low vibrational. I can't be around them."
Phrases like, "You're so much more evolved. It's not
worth your time." Phrases like, "I held too much
space. They messed with my energy field." These
are all phrases I've either used or had used on
me. And yet, I can't help but notice the way it
completely dehumanizes anyone who doesn't wear
crystals, eat vegan food, practice yoga, pull
oracle cards, or fit the modern-day elitist image
of spirituality. I love all those things, by the
way. Yet, by clinging to a specific breed of
human, am I not then excluding the very people
who I could learn the most from? The ones who
are different from me. My friends and I have
this saying, *"God is in the gutter."* And it's this
gloriously funny reminder to find the humanity
in it all instead of attempt to transcend it all.
That is the last trap. I'd rather make friends
with my demons, because there is a unique power
to a person who doesn't hide their humanity. All
of a sudden, the darkness people would normally
bury is revealed in their presence because they
subconsciously feel that all of them is welcome.
Their flaws become a badge of honor. Their hearts
a home for compassion.

As soon as I stopped searching for stable ground
I discovered I had wings
Grounding into groundlessness
Is the way of wild things

i used to avoid anything
that threw me off-center
my heart would stop at a text
and my stomach would do backflips
that could've entered me into the olympics
while my nervous system tanked faster
than the titanic
because my boundaries
were as defined as water
and my social anxiety
was my closest companion
i've chased tornados,
swam with alligators,
and leapt out of airplanes,
without a second thought
yet the minute someone invites me
to a social gathering
suddenly cuddling that alligator
sounds like a mighty fine option
because a reptile isn't going to reject me
for who i truly am
nor will it
give a damn
how awkward i am
yet i'd rather be awkward
than slip on the suit of cool
because at least i am finally
finding something
real in myself

i used to avoid anything that threw me off-center
and yet how brittle is my personal power
to avoid the very situations
that are meant to strengthen me
is my life even my own
if i am a prisoner to their approval
i am grieving
the amount of my life
i have spent not being me
i am grieving the amount of my life
i have spent not knowing
what my own voice sounds like
i am grieving the calluses on my feet
from all the eggshells i walked on
in my relationships
but if their love was really for me
then why would i morph my identity
to fit into the character in their dream
and my fear of loss only means
that i suffer twice
in this already temporary thing called life
we coddle and justify our stories
wearing them like armor
but i am not suiting up for battle anymore
i am stripping down
and bowing before no one but my own heart
nothing real can ever be destroyed
did you hear me?
this is what it means

to die before you die
kill the characters you pretended to be
my dear
die before you die
and you might just get to live
discovering what true love
really is

take the first step.
be the one who says, "i love you," first, even
if it is with a shaking voice and a thundering
heart. take the first step. be the one who
surrenders their sword of defense and meets
conflict with compassion. take the first step. be
the one who admits to their pain before throwing
up thick, cold walls. take the first step. be the
one who is direct and honest instead of speaking
behind the back of another. take the first step.
be the one who asks for help and reaches out
their hand without any thoughts of debt. take
the first step. be the one who does not enforce
their own truth, because they know there are
many truths. take the first step. the pain of
a bruised, open heart is far better than the
pain of a closed-off one that never knows true
connection. if you are to risk anything, then let
it be the risk of being yourself.

this is Love's way
to see what everyone needs
before they know they need it
where they ache to expand
i'll build an oasis
in the desert of their soul
the parts of themselves
they are too scared to touch
i'll offer a hand and get them dancing again
because my life was built on moving ground
so instability is where i become stable
i used to look for God in the stars
thinking if i could see far enough
into infinity i would find Her
how ironic
that She is closer than my jugular vein

one of the strongest trees in the world is the redwood
her roots grow so deep that even when the chaos of
  a storm hits
she does not yield
yet the seed will not germinate
until a wildfire touches it
meaning
that some of the most indestructible
forces in life are grown from the ashes
meaning
the next time you feel as though
your life is going up in flames
the path forward is clouded by smoke
and you're gasping for air
coughing up the last of your hope
but all you can breathe in is despair
remember that your struggles
are the fire you are forged from
remember that suffering only ever
deepens your cup
so there is more compassion
for the hollow hearts of this world
to drink from
remember that your spine carries
the stories of the millions of lives
that had to be lived for you to even be here
have you ever thought about that?
what a miracle it is
that you even you made it here

so stand tall
as the force of fucking nature
that you are
because beneath your feet
are the shoulders of your ancestors
and life offers no guarantees
other than the breath you're taking
so, purpose was never a question
never once did the redwood ask
if it was growing in the right direction
out of the ashes of who you once were
who will now rise?
your body is a bridge
between
death
and
life

beauty and ugly made love
and as they separated, they switched skins
this is why most of our values are backward
this is why we yearn for connection
yet isolate ourselves
this is why we seek love
but fear loss
this is why we worship what we do
but not who we are
this is why we wipe our tears away
and hide our face in shame
forgetting that every drop
that slides down our rosy cheeks
is a triumphant mark of our humanity
in a world so numb i sometimes have to check if my
  heart still beats
you see
you see
love is a double-edged sword
the part of someone that draws us in
is the part of someone that one day repels us
he loves how wild i am
how i always keep him on his toes
he loves how deeply i feel
and can turn any experience into a poem
he loves that i do well on my own
and don't rely on him to be my home
until the sword flips
he hates how wild i am

that my chaos throws him off balance
he hates how deeply i feel
and tells me i'm too dramatic
he hates that i do well on my own
and wishes i found home in him instead of alone
but isn't hate just a twisted form of love?
you see
you see
love is a double-edged sword
but you decide which blade to wield
beauty
or ugly
now i've gotten carried away
so let me explain
i hope one day
you meet the real beauty
she wears the ugly face
that gasps for air beneath that porcelain mask
she doesn't act untouchable
but boldly shows how deeply everything touches her
it may feel like you're missing several layers of
  skin
because you have finally let your sensitivity in
so next time you want to turn away
from a part of you
a part of her
a part of him
instead
lean in

i once heard that beauty fell for ugly
and if that's not the greatest love story ever told
i don't know what is

Instill enough fear in everyone
And freedom is too frightening
A luxury to maintain

you're making love to life itself. every moment is
a short eternity that we're either performing for
or melting into. it will always take a different
shape--sometimes it's slow and sometimes it's
urgent. sometimes it's tender and sometimes it's
rough. yet through all of it, the depth to which
love moves through us is the depth to which we've
found surrender. when we burn our expectations
to the ground, we've stripped down layer after
layer until we become intimate with life itself.
how you make love to your life is entirely up to
you: whether you are halfway present for it,
stumbling through each moment in an apathetic
stupor. or whether you are completely alive and
awake, married to the mystery and letting yourself
unravel in each experience. you're making love
to life itself. what will you do with your short
eternity?

A true teacher
Shakes you awake
To the understanding
That already
Slumbered within you

Burn down that house of cards
You call a reputation
Praise or blame
Will tip you off-balance
Either which way
My dear,
Who is *really* pulling your strings?

How simple it is!
Just to be here
It takes so little to fulfill
The deepest part of us
It takes so little
To look into the eyes of the "other"
And find God winking back at us
Oh, *how we bargain for our own limitations!*
Like a good lawyer
We'll find any loophole we can
To convince ourselves that we are small
As though the sun could fit
Into a small oil lamp
I can hear God laughing,
Watching as we all keep making the attempt!
Why are we so terrified of freedom?
The cost is the life we thought we needed to have
The mystic is ready to die a thousand times
Before they die
Such a fight it is
Between our two greatest desires
Freedom
And security
I hear God laughing again,
As we try to make the choice
Between the two
When security is found
By recognizing that nothing is secure!
Life is a great circle of birth and decay

Death the only winner
In the war with ourselves
So, why don't we just surrender that sword
There are flowers blooming
That need our attention
Don't sacrifice your wild at the altar of safety

when you're asking everyone
what they think you should do
that is the time
to close your mouth
open your ears
and listen to the truth
the soul has been softly
whispering to you
since the beginning
intuition > advice

i'll appear insane to them
to be sane with the beloved
i'll appear the young fool
to those who clutch knowledge
until their fingers bleed with desperation
yet know nothing of the wisdom
that emptiness brings
i'll stumble blindly
through the dark night
before i chase the light
because behind that radiant appearance
is an exaggerated shadow
Love
is beyond such things of right or wrong
because within every sinner
is a slumbering saint
and within every saint
is a sinner parched with desire
i have no interest in living a life
of quiet desperation
with a nice smile that silently begs,
"approve of me."
i'm here to dance with
all the wonderful and wicked
creatures of the world
as the earth quakes and trembles
beneath my bare feet.
so, toss aside your notions of the world
being split in black and white
meet me in that divine grey area
i'll be waiting for you
to dance with me

And if numb is the new normal, then let me be the weird one. Let me be so moved that the simple sight of dawn breaks the silence of my soul in celebration. Let me become a blank canvas for life to paint on, for I am no longer interested in drawing perfect lines to live trapped within. Let me be forever changed by the stories that tumble from your trembling lips. Let me walk down the streets feeling naked from the inside out because I am no longer covering up who I am. Let me feel all of it. The raw and chaotic richness of life because normal would forever steal the light that dances in my eyes.

i don't fall in Love
i walk in Love
one baby step at a time
because i know when it's time
i have a tendency to shove my own heart aside
my profession will become reading your moods
so, i wouldn't choose me if i were you
because dating an empath
when you don't understand your own feelings
means i will codependently try and be your healing
i'm learning boundaries
the same way i learned to play
that game jenga
i'll stack a bunch of bricks onto a wall
and hope for the best
but if you so much as breathe on them
they'll crumble into a mess
i'll give you a second chance
a hundred thousand times
but you won't get a third chance
so, i'm sorry in advance
because i'm an expert at running away
i'll disappear before you can even
ask me to stay
by the way
your heart only breaks
so that Love can rush through the cracks
and illuminate the parts of yourself
you avoided looking at

so, i no longer walk in Love
i dive headfirst
because i now understand
the birthright that is my worth

A daily prayer for you . . .

Once a day, may my worldview be shattered so
that I may never grip too tightly to any one
idea. May the glass walls that encase my mind
crumble as my perspective expands. May life
soften me, deepen me, and make me more honest
than yesterday. May I live with a heart so tender
I can truly feel the world. May my Love be
malleable and formless like water--able to
envelop everyone and let them feel free from the
weight of living for a while. May I make art that
is true, not for the result, but to awaken my soul.

have you convinced yourself
you are what you do?
sit in silence for ten days
and worthiness will never
be a question you ask again
have you convinced yourself
you are what people say you are?
spark a match to your reputation
and dance around the flames
of their praise and blame
have you convinced yourself
you are what you have?
give up what you own
until nothing owns you
even your body
is a borrowed sanctuary
let's smash that silly scale
you've been measuring your worth with
beneath our dancing feet
the best way to deal with
our friend called fear
is to call his bluff

in a dream i met the two gods of time: chronos
and kairos. chronos came from darkness and wove
together linear time to entertain himself. it is
an unstoppable current where human beings are
always going somewhere and doing something, moving
too fast and lost in their versions of reality. then
there was kairos, who was made of the light. in a
single breath, she created vertical time, where the
only thing that exists is the moment that we're in.
no illusions to be blinded by. nothing of grandeur.
just a total embrace of reality. the two of them sit
there as old friends, watching us worship them both
as we learn to tap into all there ever was, is, and
will be.

This life is but one breath in Eternity's vast,
  endless lungs . . .

She buried a treasure more precious than any gold
Knowing we would spend that one breath seeking
  every corner of the earth to possess it
But She hid it in the one place
We'd never think to look
I'll give you a hint:
Turn your gaze within

All that I have lost
Has taught me I never have anything
To begin with
Even this body
Is a borrowed sanctuary

our gifts aren't ours to keep
they are ours to give away
every unrealized piece of art
becomes a ghost
a graveyard of all the ideas
you never breathed life into
that song you never let rip free from your vocal
  cords
that poem that knocked on your rib cage
begging to be let out
that dance you refused to let rattle your bones
because you were too
cautious
careful
and realistic to spend time
believing in an invisible dream
at the end of your life
how many ghosts will haunt you?
will you have been an artist of life, a composer
  of spirit?
do not depart heavy with the weight
of all the things you could have done
let yourself return to the earth
blissfully hollow
because every last drop
of passion
of love
of magic was used

What are you holding on for? Let it all go! They'll
convince you that you need to "have it all." My God,
how heavy that would be. Your spine will nearly break
from the pressure of time, weighed down by all those
rigid expectations. Can't you see that all you were
denied was a gift, too? You're no longer too heavy
to dance. No longer surrounded by the clutter of how
you thought your life should look. Burn it all to the
ground! Cast the ashes of who you once were to the
wind. Lose yourself drunk on wonder while everyone
else scurries about trying to find purpose and
meaning. Let it all go! Hesitation draws failure like
a moth to a flame. It leaves room for them to tell
you how to live when the only compass you need beats
in your chest. Follow it with reckless abandon. Are
you going to simply tiptoe about the world, making
no sound in life? Let it all go! Better to boldly
make mistakes of your own choosing. So that when
you finally do "arrive," retiring this body, you'll
carry nothing but wild and precious memories.

To create a window where there was only a wall requires a willingness to keep reaching out your hand. Even if it trembles and shakes. Most of us require mutually assured vulnerability. We match the level of openness to the person in front of us. Connection becomes one big game of chicken. By closing off, we haven't protected ourselves from pain. No, pain will seep through the cracks of your walls regardless. All we've done is cut ourselves off from life itself. Like a bird that never leaves the nest, the wind stops whispering its secrets to her. To open is to risk. It is to shoot yourself out of the cannon, moment to moment. Safety is a silent prayer on your lips as you free-fall, but certainty is a long since forgotten hope. After all, you have wings. So, I no longer avoid the point of breaking. I say to the world, "Break my heart. Break it so wide open that all of eternity can fit in between the pieces."

make no mistake
this isn't a love poem
because
I DON'T WRITE LOVE POEMS ANYMORE . . .
but i did hear a story
about this couple
that was married for 67 years
that's 268 seasons
804 months
and 24,471 days
casual, right?
when the husband was asked
how he could be in love
with the same woman
for so long
he laughed and said,
"she hasn't been the same woman at all."
maybe that's what makes love last
to dance on the ashes
of who we once were
instead of holding each other
hostage to the person we knew
i've always feared losing you
or becoming lost in you
no one tells you
the bravest thing you can do
is open up the gates of your rib cage
and let someone leave
their fingerprints on your heart

knowing that whether
it's in a minute or a lifetime
one day you will part
but make no mistake
this isn't a love poem
because i don't write love poems anymore
but if i did
i'd tell you love may conquer all
but it will also break you until you open
to every kind of love there is
the kind of love where i'll give you my sweatshirt
  when you're cold
the kind of love where i'll kiss every wrinkle
  when you're old
the kind of love where i'll keep you on your toes
  and drive you fucking crazy but at the end of the
  day we're still lucky to call each other baby
i don't write love poems anymore
but if i did
i would say one last thing
just to make myself clear
i don't have the slightest clue what love is
but i can tell you this
it's the reason that we all exist

The world doesn't need more heroes in capes. It needs holy bandits. People who dance when the earth rumbles and quakes beneath them. People who carry keys between their teeth so the words they speak feel like coming up for air. You tried shouldering a boulder uphill, pushing toward the direction of your desires. But now, it's time to let yourself be PULLED by a gravitational force toward all that is fiercely yours to explore.

the wise ones know
our wealth is not in paper
nor is it in possessions
the greatest riches lie in nature
we receive everything we need
when we treat our planet with care
healthy reefs and rain forests
clean water and fresh air
we do not live on earth
we are made of earth
and she's calling us to help
the question is not if she will survive
it's if we will survive
the world is breaking down
so that truth can break through
and we can start asking why
it is that we do what we do
the problem isn't consumption
it's overconsumption
a belief that it's never enough
we hide our fear of death
by buying more stuff
change is here
so let's find a new way
one where balance is protected
and earth has a say

Your life is the greatest poem you will ever write

Can you hold life loosely, but also dearly? Can you
see that which you clutch the tightest, is that
which you're meant to let go of first? Can you trust
that love liberates, and never again let it be
tainted by your fear of loss, when even the Sun will
one day burn through His last flame? Can you drop
the noose of your expectations, so life has more
room to breathe? Can you burn down your hopes and
fears again and again, until all that's left is an
unshakeable trust that life itself knows exactly
where it's going? Can you cease trying to defend
your character, when you'll always be a hero or a
villain depending on what they need for their
own story? Can you treat each moment as a short
eternity, without asking if you have enough time?
Can you cradle every heartbeat like the ticking
of a precious clock, and never again sleepwalk
through your life? Can you let the world in and
feel it all, then let it go without crippling from
continuing to carry its stories on your back? Can
you laugh at disaster, yet cry at the way dawn
broke that day? Can you have the confidence to
be nothing in a world that demands you to be
everything? Can you cradle the mundane and the
mystical with equal reverence and respect? Can you
let go of everything I just said, while the words
settle into your bones so you are never haunted
by regret? Can you let your heart break so wide open,
that all of life can fit in between the pieces? Hold

life loosely and dearly, my love. Freedom is not
a goal or an attainable ability, but the humble
surrender to let life flow and dance through us.

six months later . . .

we stood in the
back of the room
with our shoulders touching
watching everyone like we had done a thousand times
laughing like we would do it
for the rest of our lives
"I still love you," he whispered
while a sea of people chattered around us
and yet those four words said more
than their endless conversations
the moment broke open
and a wave of silence rushed in
because *there were no words*
left to be spoken
"I still love you"
the words echoed through
the chamber of my heart
familiar yet foreign because
he was half family
and half stranger now
"I still love you"
I turned to him
and the room blurred around me
I saw him for the first time
without the lens of my pain
I saw the man I fell in love with
whose brilliant confidence

made anything feel possible
I saw the boy who shattered my heart
in a million pieces on the floor
because he wanted to prove
he could use a hammer
and finally
I saw a friend
one who respected
the ways we built each other
who honored what he once had
I saw all of this in half a second
and all I could do was laugh
he asked me why
and I just shook my head
"I still love you"
"of course, you idiot,"
I replied
as all our memories flashed
across my eyes
true connections never end
through time and forgiveness
the wounds all mend
but the fingerprints we leave
on each other's heart
will always remain
even if we choose to spend
our lives
forever apart

"How would you love if you were never hurt before?"
he asked.

"My love would have far less weight and depth to
it. I would never enter a relationship thinking,
'I hope I don't get hurt.' Instead, I just ask
myself: 'Is this teaching me more of what it means
to be human?' Nothing, and I mean nothing evolves
us like love."

two years later . . .

if i had one wish for you, it wouldn't be for the
kind of love they write sonnets about. a grand
fairy tale with knights and horses and battles
bled to win your heart. no, if i had one wish
for you, it would be to fall in love with your
best friend. someone you can laugh your way out
of the dark with. someone who is your biggest
cheerleader on your best days and helps you up
on your hard days. if i had one wish for you, it
would be to find a love that's stable within
its instability. someone who is strong and
unshakeable as a mountain, and you are the wild
sea whose waves collide into them in perfect
chaos. if i had one wish for you, it would be a
love that never makes you feel like you're too
much. that you couldn't possibly be too much,
because that someone has spent their whole life
seeking a person who is as gloriously enough as
you. if i had one wish for you, it would be to find
a love that is true. someone who is honest even
when it is hard and it hurts. especially then. if
i had one wish for you, it would be for a love
that is both your awakening and your undoing. a
love that is its own force. and if you're lucky,
allows you to find God mirrored in the heart of
another.

what if this was your last breath?
i'll say it again
so you really think about it
what if *this* was your last breath?
take a breath
and as your lungs taste oxygen for the final time
watch as
death unravels the fabric of your story
beneath his bony fingertips
to take an honest look
at the life that you lived
you watch with wide eyes
the chapters that unfold
revealing your mark on earth
from the first second
your body was birthed
every love and loss
trial and triumph
the pages are turning quickly now
and you beg for more time
as all of these precious moments
flash before your eyes
he pauses
and slightly turns his head
then asks you about your biggest regret
"is it that you held back in life?" he says
in a moment the truth
could have tumbled from your lips
did you water it down or swallow it?

were you brave in love?
did you give all of your heart?
or did you keep part of
it tucked away
afraid if it were seen
you'd be left alone in the dark?
were you courageous in your choices?
or did you convince yourself
comfort was the smart thing
and that was all you were capable of
as though every atom and cell in your body
wasn't an impossible love story of creation?
did you hold onto things
and let yourself be hardened
by suffering?
or did you allow forgiveness
to soften the sharp points of your pain
because all that destroyed you
was merely revealing
what was indestructible in you?
when we avoid death
we avoid life
when we avoid death
we avoid life
when we avoid death
we avoid life
"wake up,"
death whispers
as he laughs at our hesitation

because he can see
that we only occupy
a few magic seconds here
so, now there's only one page left
before you exhale that final breath
he eyes you curiously
and says,
"what would you do
if i left this page blank?
would you stay awake?
or would you let yourself be owned
by what you were afraid to face?
would you hold back?
or would you finally live the life
you wish you had?"

E

X

H

A

L

E

Acknowledgments

There are so many people I need to thank that made this book what it is. Creation is the highest form of human expression, and this art would not be as fiercely honest without the encouragement of my people. The poetry (pun intended) would otherwise remain unspoken.

To Marilyn Allen, my wonderful book agent, I am a firm believer that it only takes one "yes" for a life to change. You were my "yes" all those years ago. Thank you for your patience, encouragement, and genuine love for poetry.

To Patty Rice and the team at Andrews McMeel, I am honored that you chose to publish my work a third time. It is rare for a publisher to care in the way that the AMP crew does. Thank you, thank you, thank you.

To Dakota Adan, the Rumi to my Shamz, thank you for encouraging me to grow teeth in my work, for showing me that a poem is anything written honestly and that hope is never a fool's errand.

To Alexis Ren, I would not have survived writing this book without you. We have been so many different people together and seen each other through a thousand deaths and rebirths. Thank you for bringing me home.

To my mom, who is the most spiritually alive person I have ever met. Thank you for giving me the space to make my own mistakes and earn my wisdom, and for reading this entire book a thousand times. You're the audience I write for.

To my dad, thank you for giving me a soft place to land, for being there, no questions asked, and watering me like one of your many thriving plants. You have always been my biggest supporter, and I feel incredibly lucky to call you my dad.

To IN-Q, if I hadn't discovered your spoken word, "God Doesn't Make Mistakes," when I was fifteen, I never would have gotten into poetry. You're a master and an inspiration. Thank you for your support over the years.

To Charley Noda, without whom this title literally would not exist, you were there during my darkest hour. You listened to every single poem and sat on the porch with me for hours through the pain. When I was on my knees, you told me under no uncertain terms to get my ass up again.

To Bryan Ellis, you're the mystical joker who showed me the magic that happens when a person alchemizes their pain through art, that life really is the best, no matter what shape the moment takes. I never would have learned to break open in my spoken word without your honesty or watching you belt *"Freedom"* in my kitchen.

To Kevin Paris, thank you for playing *"Past You"* every time I asked, for recording all of those spoken words and letting me lay on your floor during the hard days. You were a safe haven.

To Jade Alectra, when we were both sick you were my anchor point. On the days I was too scared to share this, to be vulnerable, you reminded me of the power of a girl with no rib cage.

To Kayra Satya, my God I just laugh whenever I see you because we saw each other through the wildest time of our lives. You are the living expression of a woman who has the strength it takes to be soft. Cheers to many more adventures and thank you for walking out of the dark with me.

To Navi Whitten, thank you for all of the chocolate bars, for keeping me grounded when I was slipping away, and for introducing me to the Kauai end-of-life-care center, without which I never would have written the final poem in this book.

To Anfisa Kuzmina, your patience is unparalleled. Thank you for bringing my poems to life with your art, for understanding the heartbeat of the words without me having to explain. Cheers to many more creative projects! I cannot wait to see your pieces in a gallery someday soon.

To my We Are Warriors girls, our weekly calls are my favorite part of the week. Getting to hear your stories, watch you grow, and make beautiful things is an immeasurable honor. I love you. To us, and to more poetry and intense breathwork sessions!

To my readers, I believe our time and energy is the most precious gift we can give someone. I don't take it lightly. Your love and support means the world. Every workshop, message, or conversation helps me understand just how connected we are and gives me great hope for the future of our world. All I can say is keep going, despite there being nowhere to arrive.

About the Author

Allie Michelle is a two-time bestselling author and spoken word artist. Her two poetry collections hit number one in poetry within the first week of release, and she has had several viral spoken word videos amassing millions of views. Allie is the co-founder of holistic wellness school We Are Warriors. She has also recently launched an NFT drop called Sirens, a women-run project investing in building a sustainable mental health retreat center. Allie spent years traveling the globe, studying somatic release and how to help people find balance in their bodies. She is a certified yoga, breathwork, meditation, reiki, and craniosacral therapist. Her goal is to teach people tools that help them connect with themselves, so they can become a vessel rather than a victim. Allie continues to this day to dedicate her gifts to bringing out the gifts in others.